Historic

Postcards

from

Old Kansas City

COMPILED AND EDITED BY
MICHAEL G. BUSHNELL

ACKNOWLEDGMENTS: TRACY ABELN, MELISSA HEALER

ISBN:1-58597-200-2

LIBRARY OF CONGRESS CONTROL NUMBER: 2003112205

A DIVISION OF SQUIRE PUBLISHERS, INC.
4500 COLLEGE BLVD.
LEAWOOD, KS 66211
1/888/888-7696
WWW.LEATHERSPUBLISHING.COM

To my wife, Christine, whose grace, love and patience still amaze me.
And to my late mother, Agnes, who taught me to Smile — it makes people wonder
what you're up to, and that while all that glitters may not be gold,
if you look closer, there's usually a lesson to be learned.

FOREWORD

As a public communications medium, postcards essentially began during the Columbian Exposition in Chicago Illinois, May 1893. Illustrations of exhibits at the Exposition were printed on government-issued postal cards and on privately printed souvenir cards. The writing of personal messages on the cards was prohibited on the address side, which required a 2-cent stamp. Later, in 1898, Congress passed an act creating the private mailing Card, which required a 1-cent stamp to mail. After 1901, when the government allowed the word "POST CARD" to be printed on the back of the card, citizens actually were able to make their own postcards by mounting their black & white photos on paper with postcard backs. It was not until 1907, when the "divided back" style of postcard became popular, that messages written on one side of the back of the card were allowed by the government. At that time, postcards were printed almost exclusively in Germany, due to the Germans' superiority in color lithographic processes at the time. The advent of the First World War, however, transferred printing of postcards to England or to printers here in the United States. During the 1930s, new printing processes were introduced that allowed the printing of postcards on heavy paper with a high rag content, causing a finish resembling that of fine linen. Print costs were extremely cheap, which allowed for the use of brightly colored inks. Finally, in 1945, "Photo-Chrome" postcards began to overtake the older linen style cards in popularity. Photo-Chrome cards can be seen on most any postcard sales rack across the country today.

In 1990, I purchased a home in the heart of Kansas City's Historic Northeast area. The home was originally built in 1901 for J.W. Lyman, a prominent Kansas City Republican. It was at this time that I developed a passion for all things old, including old Kansas City postcards. After acquiring The Northeast News in July 1998, my wife and I decided to include postcards as a weekly feature of the paper, originally running a different card from the Historic Northeast every week. As time progressed, we decided to include historic postcards showing views from all over the Kansas City metropolitan area. What you see on these pages is a compilation of cards from the first four years of our ownership of The Northeast News. We hope you enjoy them as much as we have enjoyed researching each view and transcribing the messages scrawled on the backs to friends and loved ones. These endearing messages updated each other on everything from health and marital status to the price of hogs and grain in the Kansas City market. Enjoy!

~ Michael

Historic Postcards from Old Kansas City

Anyone interested in traveling to Atlantic City to visit the Boardwalk or romp in the surf needed to travel no further than the 4200 block of N. Chouteau Trafficway during the 1920s and 1930s. Known as the "Atlantic City of the West," Winwood Beach was a place to kick up your heels and relax for the weekend. Today, the entire site is occupied by the Chouteau Crossings Shopping Center. No evidence of the beach, the amusement park or the lake exist any longer. This postcard was mailed to Miss Elsie Buttenbach of Long Beach, New Jersey on October 27, 1931. It reads: "Still enjoying the sights. How would you like to be along, seeing the country with both eyes? Greetings from W. Bill."

"The Atlantic City of the West"

A REGULAR SUNDAY CROWD, WINWOOD BEACH, KANSAS CITY, MO.

HISTORIC POSTCARDS FROM OLD KANSAS CITY

THE OMAR LOUNGE IN THE CONTINENTAL HOTEL WAS JUST ONE OF MANY PLACES TO SEE AND BE SEEN DURING THE EVENING HOURS IN THE 1930S AND 1940S. FORMER KMBC RADIO "TOWER ADORBLE" MARY JANE DANIELS (COLEMAN), ALSO KNOWN AS MARY JANE THOMPSON AT KMBC RADIO (SPECIFICALLY, THE JOANN TAYLOR RADIO SHOW), OFTEN SPEAKS FONDLY ABOUT LIFE IN KANSAS CITY DURING THE 1940S: "THERE WAS THE OMAR LOUNGE, THEN IN THE PHILLIPS THERE WAS THE TROPICS AND THE CABANA, AND THE MUEHLEBACH HAD THE CAFE TRIANON AND THE TERRACE GRILL. OF COURSE, THE HOTEL PRESIDENT HAD THE DRUM ROOM. DOWNTOWN WAS THE PLACE TO BE BECAUSE EVERYONE WENT THERE!" THE DESCRIPTION ON THE BACK OF THIS POSTCARD READS: "AIR CONDITIONED. THE OMAR OFFERS A FESTIVE MOOD, ENHANCED BY SMART ENVIRONMENT, RESPONDS TO THE GAY ATMOSPHERE OF HAPPY PEOPLE. THIS DELIGHTFUL ROOM INVITES LEISURELY ENJOYMENT OF TALENTED MUSICIANS AND THE WIDEST SELECTIONS OF THE WORLD'S CHOICEST BEVERAGES."

Historic Postcards from Old Kansas City

Elmwood Cemetery is present home to 11 of Kansas City's Mayors and its First Police Chief, Thomas Speers. Speers was known to associate with other lawmen of note, including Wild Bill Hickock. This card, published by the Southwest News Company of Kansas City, Missouri, shows the stately gates and the entrance to the Historic Cemetery. In recent years, the Cemetery has sponsored Civil War re-enactments and various other historic programs. Some of Kansas City's earliest families of note lie in peace in the confines of Elmwood's walls. Some names of note include Kirkland B. Armour, Kersey Coates, Jacob Loose and Thomas Bullene. This card was sent to a Mrs. Rose Rutherford of LaPorte, Colorado (directly N.W. of Fort Collins) in 1911. It reads: "Dear Rose, No I do not take the Journal. I just posted a letter to you a few minutes before I got your letter. Ella." According to Bill Winbigler, present curator of Elmwood, over 35,000 people are buried there. The entire cemetery is listed on the National Register of Historic Places due to the large number of past city officials interred there. The cemetery, founded in 1872, is located at 15th and Elmwood, "Where Kansas City's Past Is Buried."

Elmwood Cemetery.   Kansas City, Mo.

HISTORIC POSTCARDS FROM OLD KANSAS CITY

THE DESCRIPTION ON THE BACK OF THIS LINEN TYPE POSTCARD, PUBLISHED BY MAX BERNSTEIN OF KANSAS CITY, MO., READS, "FIVE MINUTES BY AUTOMOBILE FROM THE DOWNTOWN BUSINESS DISTRICT IS KANSAS CITY'S MUNICIPAL AIRPORT, WITH THE FINE TERMINAL BUILDING PICTURED. THREE AIRLINES, TRANSCONTINENTAL & WESTERN AIR, MID-CONTINENT AIR AND BRANIFF AIRWAYS HAVE FIFTY-FOUR SCHEDULES IN AND OUT OF KANSAS CITY DAILY. TWENTY-SEVEN ARRIVALS AND TWENTY-SEVEN DEPARTURES." PASSENGER SERVICE AT OLD MUNICIPAL BEGAN IN SEPTEMBER 1927. KANSAS CITY BOUGHT THE SWAMPY AIRPORT SITE IN 1926, AND CHARLES LINDBERGH DEDICATED THE AIRPORT, WITH THOUSANDS ATTENDING, IN AUGUST 1927. AN OPEN AIR DECK ON THE SECOND LEVEL OF THE TERMINAL BUILDING ALLOWED PEOPLE TO WATCH TAKE OFFS AND LANDINGS OF THE BIG PLANES. THIS WAS A COMMON SCENE IN DAYS WHEN FLYING WAS STILL A MARVEL. A RESTAURANT, WHICH OPENED INSIDE LATER, ADDED TO A GALA OUTING AT THE AIRPORT. THE PRESENT KANSAS CITY INTERNATIONAL AIRPORT, IN KANSAS CITY NORTH, WAS FINANCED BY CITY BONDS IN 1966 AND DEDICATED IN 1972.

TERMINAL BUILDING, AT AIRPORT, WITH SKYLINE IN BACKGROUND, KANSAS CITY, MO.

HISTORIC POSTCARDS FROM OLD KANSAS CITY

KERSEY COATES DRIVE, AS SHOWN IN THIS MAX BERNSTEIN POSTCARD FROM THE MID-1920S, HUGGED THE FACE OF THE CLIFF BETWEEN 17TH STREET AND CLARK'S POINT. IT WAS SUSPENDED ON A BOULEVARD MIDWAY BETWEEN THE TOP AND BOTTOM OF THE CLIFF SO THAT IT APPEARED FORBIDDING TO THOSE ARRIVING BY TRAIN AT THE UNION DEPOT IN THE WEST BOTTOMS. KERSEY COATES DRIVE LAY ALONG WEST TERRACE PARK, AND TREES, SHRUBS AND VINES WERE PLANTED IN PROFUSION IN 1908 WHEN THE LOOKOUT TOWERS AND STEPS WERE BUILT ABOVE THE DRIVE AT TENTH AND THE BLUFF. KERSEY COATES DRIVE WAS NAMED FOR KERSEY COATES, A PENNSYLVANIA QUAKER WHO ARRIVED IN KANSAS CITY IN THE 1850S AND WAS AN EARLY PROPONENT OF WHAT WAS THEN CALLED THE TOWN OF KANSAS. TODAY, THE WESTERN PORTION OF THE DOWNTOWN LOOP RUNS ALONG THE SAME HILLSIDE AS THE SCENIC DRIVE ONCE DID. MOST OF THE STONEWORK IS STILL INTACT, INCLUDING THE TWIN STONE TOWERS OVERLOOKING THE WEST BOTTOMS, AND SOME OF THE STEPS.

65:—Palisades, Kersey Coates Drive, Kansas City, Mo.

HISTORIC POSTCARDS FROM OLD KANSAS CITY

SENT IN APRIL 1910, THIS POSTCARD, PUBLISHED BY S.H. KNOX OF KANSAS CITY AND DEPICTING "THE WHITE SQUADRON, ELECTRIC PARK, KANSAS CITY, MISSOURI," SHOWS A BEVY OF PEOPLE ENJOYING AN OUTING ON THE LAKE AT ELECTRIC PARK. THE PARK WAS ORIGINALLY BUILT BY THE HEIM BROTHERS NEAR THEIR BREWERY AT THE FOOT OF CHESTNUT AVENUE IN THE EAST BOTTOMS. IT WAS MOVED IN 1906 TO THE THEN-CITY LIMITS NEAR 47TH AND THE PASEO. THE MESSAGE ON THE BACK OF THE CARD INDICATES IT WAS SENT TO MISS VIRGINIA CAMPBELL OF NORTH JEFFERSON STREET IN MARSHALL, MO. THE MESSAGE READS: "DEAR LITTLE LADY, DIDN'T GET TO SEE YOU VERY LONG, BUT CERTAINLY THOUGHT YOU A DEAR SWEET LITTLE DARLING. HOW WISH COULD SEE YOU OFTEN. DID YOU KISS PAPA GOOD-BYE FOR AUNT MOLLIE? WRITE TO ME SOMETIME."

The White Squadron, Electric Park, Kansas City, Mo.

Historic Postcards from Old Kansas City

This Real Photo postcard was published by the North American Postcard Company of Kansas City, Missouri. It shows one of Kansas City's famous street cars trundling down Walnut Street, between 10TH & 11TH streets. Some prominent businesses in the background include Woolf Brothers, Olney Music Company and Taft's Dental Rooms. This card shows a woman pausing outside Woolf Brothers which, interestingly enough, was an all male establishment at the time, featuring men's custom-made shirts as a leading seller of the day.

648—Walnut St looking North
Kansas City Mo

Historic Postcards from Old Kansas City

The American Legion fountain, dedicated Nov. 3, 1921, at Ninth and Main, is pictured on an old post card published in black and white in France, by Jno. Straley. Straley published a whole series of postcards of Kansas City during the early 1920s and 1930s from his apartment at 213 N. Mersington Ave. The fountain's dedication ceremonies took place during the 1921 American Legion convention in Kansas City, which was attended by 60,000 veterans and the five military leaders of World War I: Beatty, Foch, Jacques, Pershing and Diaz. Robert M. Gage, noted Kansas City sculptor, designed the stone memorial and fountain. Gage's design includes bronze Friezes of "doughboys" of World War I in action, recessed into a pillar topped by four eagles. Today the memorial is located at the Budd Park Esplanade, on the east side of Van Brunt Boulevard at Anderson. A list of Kansas City American Legion Posts named for men who gave their lives is on the monument, but time and erosion have made deciphering difficult. The inscription is as follows: "Dedicated by Kansas City to the American Legion Posts, October 31-November, 1921. William T. Fitzsimmons, Murray Davis, William J. Bland, Joseph Dillon, Arthur Maloney, Sanford M. Brown Jr., James Cummins, Joseph Liebman, Hewitt Swearingen, Wayne Minor." The fountain was severely damaged in 2001 by a hit-and-run driver. Efforts to restore the fountain are currently being explored by The Parks Department and area business people.

KANSAS CITY, MO.
American Legion Fountain
Ninth and Main Streets

Historic Postcards from Old Kansas City

The Home Rug and Curtain Cleaning Company, located at 4724-32 Forest Avenue. Branch office located at 4729 Troost. (Troost and Forest are one block apart.) "Equipped with the latest equipment for taking care of all garments, household furnishings, furniture repairing and upholstering." This is a linen card, circa 1940s, and published by Curt Teich of Chicago, Illinois. The building shown on the card is still standing.

"Perfect Garment Cleaning"

HOME RUG & CURTAIN CLEANING CO. — KANSAS CITY, MO.   4A-H1777

Historic Postcards from Old Kansas City

In 1908, probably the last thing on anyone's mind, especially these young cadets of the Kansas City Fire Department, was a war of any kind. The caption reads, "A few of the bravest, Kansas City Fire Department, Kansas City, Missouri." This card was sent to Miss Effie Rodell of 1105 Vermont St., Lawrence, Kan. It reads, " Hello Miss Rodell. Everything is lovely. Miss you so much. Hope you enjoy your vacation. Will see a few of our brave boys out back later. Love, from all the girls. Lovingly, Grace." It was mailed on July 25, 1908 at 11 a.m. A fitting honor for those brave men and women who serve our city and country.

Historic Postcards from Old Kansas City

The City Workhouse, located at 2001 Vine, was built in the late 1860s and was used by the city from 1872 through the late 1960s. Often described as "the castle," the structure was used to house violators of municipal ordinances. The long wing on the left contained cells where prisoners were housed. A platform where an armed guard stood is still visible today on the decaying structure. Armed guards took positions on the platform until 1911, when the male prisoners were transferred to new facilities at Leeds. Only women prisoners occupied the facility after that. Most recently, the building was used by the Water department as a storage facility. This card, published by the Southwest News Company, was sent to Mrs. Alice Brister of New Orleans, Louisiana. It reads, "Dear Alice, I leave for home on Saturday. Have had a fine visit with Morton. Alice is up and looks real well. Morton is fine. Fred was here three days. Weather very warm. All our love, Aunt Alice." It was mailed on August 7, 1907.

Workhouse, Kansas City, Mo.

Historic Postcards from Old Kansas City

Traditionally in high gear in Kansas City throughout the month of October, this card is from the American Royal from days gone by, and features the Swift & Company Prize Draft Team. It is dated October 10 to 13, 1906. It was mailed to Miss Cora Rhoades of Rural Route 1 in Wellsville, Kan. The American Royal Horse Show, according to the late Russell Sage Sr., architect for the Kansas City Stock Yards Co., began in 1899. A first board of directors of the American Royal is to be found in the minutes of a meeting held March 2, 1904, when the following officers were elected: C.A. Standard, Emporia, Kan., president; T.J. Wornall (a shorthorn cattle breeder), Liberty, Mo., secretary; C.R. Thomas, Kansas City, general manager; H.W. Elliot, Estil, Mo., E.P. Weld, Ovid, Mo. and M.H. Gentry, Sedalia, Mo., vice presidents, and Allen Thompson, Nashua, Mo., superintendent. (The late Allen Thompson was the father of Mrs. Jay Dillingham.)

AMERICAN ROYAL LIVE STOCK SHOW, KANSAS CITY, KAS.

OCTOBER 10TH TO 13TH, 1906.

Swift & Company Prize Draft Team

Ask Your Dealer for Swift's Premium Hams and Bacon.

Friday night.

Oct. 12, 1906

Souvenir of American Royal.

Historic Postcards from Old Kansas City

You might say that railroading was a passion for Fred Harvey. So much so that he developed a chain of restaurants in and around train stations across the country. This postcard, published by Fred Harvey, shows the new Santa Fe Railroad bridge across the Missouri River at Sibley, Missouri. The description on the back states: "Experts and engineers have come from all parts of the country and from Europe to see the bridge the Santa Fe has recently completed at Sibley, Mo. The new bridge was built on enlarged piers of the old structure and the old bridge removed without delaying traffic a single minute, a feat which, considering the large and heavy construction, marks an epoch in recent engineering achievement. The new bridge is three times as heavy as the old one, is over 4000 feet long and cost a million and a quarter dollars." The card is a white border postcard, published between 1919 and 1930.

H-2428 NEW SANTA FE BRIDGE OVER THE MISSOURI RIVER, SIBLEY, MO. Copr. Fred Harvey.

Historic Postcards from Old Kansas City

"Keep Fit for only $8.50 per month! For a complete conditioning program, Felldman-Hirsch Health Club, 1017 Grand Avenue. Phone VI-5638-9. The presentation of this card entitles the bearer to one demonstration." So says this advertising postcard mailed to Dr. G.J. Conley at the old Lakeside Hospital, 29th and Flora, Kansas City. Both J.C. Hirsch and Edw. Feldman are pictured on the front of the card, which also shows photos of people (mostly men) relaxing on the "Out-Door Sun-Roof" or taking part in "individual excercise" programs. Noted as "Kansas City's Leading Health Club," they were Certainly ahead of their time.

KANSAS CITY'S LEADING HEALTH CLUB

J. C. Hirsch   Individual Exercise   On the Sun-Roof   Individual Exercise   Edw. Felldman

Out-Door Sun Roof

FELLDMAN-HIRSCH HEALTH CLUB - 1017 Grand Ave., Kansas City, Mo.

Historic Postcards from Old Kansas City

The Concourse Entrance to Cliff Drive on a postcard published by the Elite Postcard Company of Kansas City, Mo. This view is actually at the top of what is affectionately known as "The Gooseneck," looking south on Gladstone Boulevard toward the Concourse. A number of automobiles of the day, as well as carriages, are shown making their way along Gladstone, probably out for a leisurely drive in the park. North Terrace Park, of which the Concourse and Cliff Drive are all a part, was the brainchild of landscape architect George Kessler. The drive was actually built in sections and was totally completed in the late 1920s. It was heralded across the midwest as one of the most beautiful drives in the country. The view today from this vantage point has changed little. The addition of a few houses along the east end of Gladstone is the only minor change in this view. The card was sent to Mr. Floyd Fickel, Rural Route 5, Paola, Kan. on May 10, 1911 by a woman named Elsie who resided at 3766 Mercier, Kansas City, Mo.

Concourse, Entrance to Cliff Drive, Kansas City, Mo.

Historic Postcards from Old Kansas City

This card shows the 15th Street entrance to Mt. Washington Park. Mt. Washington Park was a project of Willard E. Winner and occupied part of Winner's 2,400 acres of woods and streams between Kansas City and Independence. A dam was built by Winner in 1887, and the newly created 20-acre lake was named Swan Lake for the graceful birds who made the lake their home. Local trains, cable car lines and later electric street car lines carried park patrons to the grounds where boating, swimming, picnic facilities, concessions, rides, band concerts and even opera were available during the summer. In 1900, at the park's closing, about 400 acres of the park were purchased by the Mount Washington Cemetery Association, formed by a group of prominent Kansas Citians. A handsome 1902 pictorial brochure issued by the Union Note Bank Company lists the 100 "gentlemen" who incorporated themselves into the cemetery association and stated: "Under the direction of Mr. George E. Kessler the grounds are being laid out on a most elaborate and extensive scale. It is expected the grounds will be opened to the public in the summer of 1902. Mount Washington will become one of the most noted cemeteries in the United States, it having so many natural advantages and under the skillful treatment as directed by Mr. Kessler, who has at his disposal the necessary funds to carry out his ideas."

Fifteenth Street Entrance, Mt. Washington Cemetery, Kansas City, Mo.

Historic Postcards from Old Kansas City

"View of one of the principal business thoroughfares. Kansas City and suburbs has a population of 500,000; ranks fifth in bank clearings and is known as the most thriving city in the Middle West." According to the legend on the back of this pre-linen postcard published by the E.C. Kropp Company of Milwaukee Wisconsin, "Kansas City retains the name of its Main Street so named back in frontier days, when covered wagons rumbled along the then dusty path. Today it is a busy, hustling thoroughfare." To the left is the F.W. Woolworth store, where almost anything could be had for a nickel or a dime. Peck's Dry Goods store is on the corner, and Harzfelds is farther down the block on the left.

MAIN STREET, LOOKING SOUTH FROM 11TH STREET, KANSAS CITY, MO.—23

"THE HEART OF THE BUSIEST SHOPPING CENTER"

Historic Postcards from Old Kansas City

The cliffs located in Historic Northeast Kansas City offered noted Landscape architect George Kessler a great challenge. Kessler, for whom the park is named, had a great dream of developing Kansas City's natural terrain and natural beauty with parks and boulevards encircling the entire city. With the backing of the City's first Parks Board, Kessler set to work on Cliff Drive. The first section of the drive was completed and opened to the public in 1900. It meandered through the wooded hills of then named North Terrace Park. Pictures taken during the drive's construction show laborers using horse and mule teams to haul rock and dirt for the completion of the drive. Later, the drive was lit by gaslights, spaced about 100 feet apart, lighting both the drive and its four approaches. In a letter to the park board, Kessler wrote: "We are charged with the duty of developing a plan that shall not only meet present, but future wants." This real photo postcard, published by the North American Post Card Company of Kansas City, was mailed from Kansas City, Mo. to Miss Carrie Webster of Los Angeles, Calif. on Sept.10, 1910.

Historic Postcards from Old Kansas City

Southwest News Company published thousands of postcards around the turn of the nineteeth century showing various views of the Kansas City area. This undivided back card shows Grand Avenue looking south from Eighth Street. An uncolored photo view card, it shows the old Federal Building at the southeast corner of Eighth and Grand. Farther south on the east side of Grand is the Jacoby Furniture Company. Across the street is a sign for the MKT (Missouri, Kansas, and Texas, better known as "The Katy") Railroad. The old Federal Building was razed in the 1930s to make way for a newer courthouse on the same site. That building was used until late in 1998 when the new facility was finished at Eighth and Oak. This card was sent to Mr. William Kenner of Holgate, Ohio from S.M. House of Grain Valley, Missouri in 1908. It reads, "I teach an ungraded school and read normal instructors. Will be pleased to exchange postals. S.M. House."

Grand Avenue South from 8th St. Kansas City, Mo.

Historic Postcards from Old Kansas City

Built in 1916 at a cost of roughly $400,000, the "new" Westgate Hotel was billed as a moderately priced hostelry for "cattlemen, small town merchants, and traveling men of limited income." The building replaced the old Vaughn's Diamond, originally erected on the site in 1869. The hotel, built of reinforced concrete and terra cotta, was operated by Elmer Williams and his brother and had 200 rooms, each featuring a private bath. Rates for the hotel ranged from $1.50 - $2.00 per day. Later, the Hotel was sold and re-named the Hotel Kay. Ultimately, it was razed in 1954 to accomodate "modern traffic needs." Today, a statue of "The Muse of the Missouri" stands on the site, surrounded by modern office buildings.

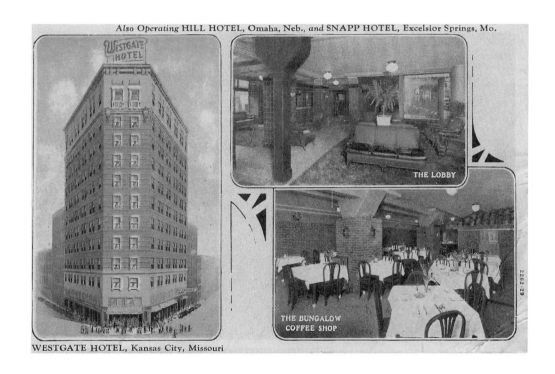

Also Operating HILL HOTEL, Omaha, Neb., and SNAPP HOTEL, Excelsior Springs, Mo.

THE LOBBY

THE BUNGALOW COFFEE SHOP

WESTGATE HOTEL, Kansas City, Missouri

HISTORIC POSTCARDS FROM OLD KANSAS CITY

THE FIRST ELECTRIC PARK WAS OPENED BY THE HEIM BROTHERS NEAR THE FOOT OF WHAT IS NOW CHESTNUT TRAFFICWAY IN KANSAS CITY'S EAST BOTTOMS. ADMISSION TO THE PARK WAS A MERE 10 CENTS. IN 1907, HOWEVER, THE BROTHERS DECIDED TO MOVE THEIR PARK TO THE SOUTHERN REACHES OF THE CITY AT 46TH & THE PASEO. ON MAY 19, 1907, THE NEW ELECTRIC PARK WAS CHRISTENED. NAMED FOR ITS 100,000 ELECTRIC LIGHT BULBS OUTLINING BUILDINGS AND RIDES, ELECTRIC PARK WAS DUBBED "THE GREAT WHITE CITY OF BRUSH CREEK." BREWERS BY TRADE, THE HEIMS OFFERED NO BEER IN THEIR PARK AS CITY FATHERS REFUSED THEM A LICENSE, DESPITE THE PARK BEING ON THEIR PREMISES. SOON, HOWEVER, THE RETURNS FROM RIDES, FOOD AND SHOOTING GALLERIES WERE SO GREAT THAT THE BEER ISSUE FADED INTO MEMORY. NOT TO BE OUT HOODWINKED BY THE CITY FATHERS THOUGH, THE BROTHERS HEIM PLACED A ONE-PENNY SURCHARGE ON GLASSES OF WATER. WHILE THERE WAS A CHARGE FOR SWIMMING, THERE WAS NO CHARGE FOR THE NIGHT SPECTACLE OF "LIVING STATUARY" AT THE FOUNTAIN IN THE LAKE. AS IF BY MAGIC, BEAUTIFUL YOUNG WOMEN EMERGED FROM THE FOUNTAIN EACH HOUR OF THE EVENING. THE WOMEN WERE FLOODED WITH COLORED LIGHT AND CROWDS WERE ENTRANCED BY THE SIGHT. SADLY, A LARGE PORTION OF THE PARK BURNED IN 1925 AND WAS NOT REBUILT. TIMES BEGAN TO CHANGE AS THE AUTOMOBILE, MOVIES AND RADIO ALL COMPETED FOR THE PUBLIC'S DOLLARS AND TIME. EVENTUALLY, THE SKELETON OF THE COASTER WAS FINALLY TORN DOWN IN THE 1940S AND THE VILLAGE GREEN APARTMENTS WERE BUILT ON THE SITE IN 1948. NO TRACES OF THE PARK EXIST TODAY.

The Chutes — Electric Park, Kansas City, Mo.

Historic Postcards from Old Kansas City

This is a linen postcard of Kenney's Harley-Davidson, located at 403 Southwest Blvd. Now Wayne's House of Choppers, owned by Wayne and Jerry Winters, this is the oldest motorcycle shop in Kansas City. Its roots date back to 1918 when the operation was converted from a livery stable. According to Wayne Winters Jr., a manual lift still exists in the back of an outbuilding where horses were actually lowered into the basement stables for feeding and keeping. From 1918 until 1947, the dealership was owned by Eddie Whitman. Then in 1947, the dealership was sold to Kenney's and it remained an authorized Harley-Davidson dealer until Wayne Winters Sr. bought Kenney out and changed the name to Wayne's House of Choppers. Today, the shop is home to one of the most extensive antique Harley parts lines in the city, featuring parts for Knuckleheads, Panheads, Shovelheads and Evolution motors. The longtime dealer has been featured in articles in both the Kansas City Star and the Kansas City Business Journal. The description on the back indicates that "Kenney's carries the entire family of Harley-Davidson Motorcycles." This card was never mailed.

Historic Postcards from Old Kansas City

Kansas City's Missouri River Front is pictured in this old turn-of-the-century postcard published by The Southwest News Company of Kansas City. In the mid-1800s, Missouri River steamboat passengers who were California bound disembarked at the great bend in the river and continued their westward journey by wagon train. Some pioneers abandoned plans for the arduous overland trip and settled in the town of Kansas. Upriver, between what is now Riverside and Parkville, is the site of old Fort Quindaro. Today, little is known or remains of the town named for Quindaro Brown, a Wyandott Indian of royal blood, who became Mrs. Abelard Guthrie (Guthrie was a member of the original town company of Quindaro). The town, surveyed by O.A. Bassett, was bounded on the north by the Missouri River and extended far enough back to average about three-fourths of a mile in width. This card pictures the skyline of downtown Kansas City circa 1908. In the far left of the picture is the Hannibal Bridge. It was built in 1869 and was the first railroad bridge across the Missouri River. In the center of the picture, the Board of Trade building can be seen as well. This photo was taken from the point where the Kansas and Missouri rivers connect. A large rock bearing the names of Lewis and Clark marks the spot today. (Getting to it is another story, as it is fenced off by the Kansas City Water Works plant!)

Kansas City~Missouri River Front, Kansas City, Mo.

Historic Postcards from Old Kansas City

This real photo postcard was published by the North American Postcard Company of Kansas City, Missouri. It shows the 12th Street viaduct under construction, leading from above Kersey Coates Drive to the West Bottoms. The viaduct opened on March 18, 1915. A story in the morning paper indicated that, "A municipal dream of years was realized this morning. The 12th Street Viaduct was opened to traffic." At 5:30 a.m. when the first car was routed over the massive new bridge, it was still dark outside. Motormen from the various car lines had requested to be the one to route the first car over the new span. However, officials decided to route cars by schedule. The first car slowly entered upon the new rails of the big double-decker bridge, gained speed and soon was at the curve at Liberty Street in the West Bottoms. The bridge is of reinforced concrete construction and was built by the Graff Construction Co. at a cost of approximately $650,000. The length of the upper deck is 2,278 feet. The lower deck is 1,884 feet. The highest point is 118 feet and the width of the roadway is 30 feet. The viaduct is still in use today and is currently under evaluation for repairs.

WEST 12TH ST. TRAFFIC WAY.

Historic Postcards from Old Kansas City

It is doubtful that the West Bottoms (Central Industrial District) have changed much since this picture postcard was made in the late 1900s. This card shows the newly constructed Inter-City Viaduct, spanning the oft-flooded area at the confluence of the Kansas and Missouri rivers. This card shows the viaduct linking Kansas City, Missouri and Kansas City, Kansas. For a number of years, it was municipally owned, and a small toll was collected to offset construction and maintenance costs. (A novel idea, don't you think!) The absence of a levy is obvious as the encroachment of the river is clearly evident in the picture. Railroads often had to re-route train traffic due to the then untamed waters of the Missouri River. This card was sent to F. N. Brunsen of Guthrie, Iowa on December 14, 1921. It reads, "Dear Uncle Frank. Headed home to K.C. I bet you play on this viaduct. There aren't any walls on it so men are un-restricted. I will write you a real letter soon. I have to go to my French now, so this is short and happy. Love, your Niece, Eloise Bierly."

Inter-City Viaduct, Kansas City, Mo.

Historic Postcards from Old Kansas City

Located on 9TH street between Oak & McGee, the Hotel Victoria was considered a "fine and substantial hotel" when it originally opened in 1888. Especially popular with cattlemen, it was often used as a place to conduct agri-buisiness transactions. Built by George Holmes, it was opened in May 1888 and boasted 240 rooms, all parlor and bedroom suites with a bath for each suite. Other hostelries of the day had bathroom facilities located "down the hall," but the Victoria was first with "privacy for all." According to city records, the building was destroyed by fire during February 1960. According to newspaper accounts, firemen and equipment were all covered with icicles, creating an eerie scene in contrast to the flames. Thirty-five people were evacuated from the hotel as fire crews fought in vain to save the almost century-old structure. A surface parking lot occupies the site today.

Cafe, Hotel Victoria.

Historic Postcards from Old Kansas City

"On Cliff Drive, Kansas City, Mo." is the description on this card published by the E.C. Kropp Company of Milwaukee, Wis. The photo was taken in the late teens or the early 1920s, and shows "gridlock" on Cliff Drive. A testament to the drive's popularity even then, hundreds of cars can be seen double-, even triple-parked along the roadway. In the distance, in the heart of the East Bottoms area, the Heim Brewery building can be seen along the horizon. Cliff Drive was the place to see and be seen in the early 1900s and remains a beautiful spot to walk, drive, cycle or run today. With the addition of Scenic Byway status, Cliff Drive enjoys a renewed popularity, as well as additional attention from local and state agencies. Numerous improvements are currently on the drawing board for the Cliff Drive Corridor, all designed to renew and restore interest in one of the nation's most beautiful byways.

ON CLIFF DRIVE, KANSAS CITY, MO.

HISTORIC POSTCARDS FROM OLD KANSAS CITY

THIS REAL PHOTO POSTCARD, PUBLISHED BY THE NORTH AMERICAN POSTCARD COMPANY OF KANSAS CITY, MISSOURI, SHOWS THE TOWERS AT 10TH STREET, OVERLOOKING KERSEY COATES DRIVE. THE DRIVE RAN ALONG THE FACE OF THE RUGGED WEST BLUFF THAT OVERLOOKED THE STOCK YARDS AND THE CENTRAL INDUSTRIAL DISTRICT. IT RAN BETWEEN 17TH STREET AND CLARK'S POINT AND APPEARED QUITE FORBIDDING TO THOSE ARRIVING AT THE OLD UNION DEPOT. DESIGNED BY NOTED LANDSCAPE ARCHITECT GEORGE KESSLER, WEST TERRACE PARK AND COATES DRIVE REPLACED AN UGLY HILLSIDE OF SHANTIES AND BILLBOARDS. THE CITY FATHERS THOUGHT IT BEST TO DESIGN SOMETHING MORE AESTHETICALLY PLEASING TO THE NEW ARRIVALS TAKING THE NINTH STREET INCLINE RAILWAY INTO DOWNTOWN. A SERIES OF STEPS AND SIDEWALKS LINKED THE DRIVE BELOW TO THE TOWERS ABOVE. FROM THE TOWERS, A PANORAMIC VIEW OF ALL POINTS NORTH AND WEST STILL EXISTS TODAY.

Historic Postcards from Old Kansas City

This scene depicts the Ft. Leavenworth Interurban Depot, circa 1911 or so. The car is loaded with soldiers, awaiting the beginning of their ride to the P.X. (Post Exchange) on base, downtown Leavenworth, or maybe even a big trip to Kansas City. In 1914, Kansas City was served by no less than eight interurban lines, connecting St. Joseph, Excelsior Springs and all points in between. Over two million passengers rode the lines each year, being the primary mode of transportation at that time. Surprisingly, a majority of the buildings shown in this card still stand today. The depot still stands, but has been adaptively re-used as a community center for families living on base. In the background, officers' quarters can be seen, which still are used today. Sadly, a majority of the interurban lines discontinued use in the mid-1930s. The increased production of the automobile, as well as buses, hard-surfaced roads and the Depression all exacted their toll on the lines.

5658. Car Station, Fort Leavenworth, Kansas.

Historic Postcards from Old Kansas City

The Liberty Memorial, Kansas City's largest monument, is pictured in a dramatic scene on a linen, color postcard published for the Allis Press in Kansas City in the 1940s. The legend on the reverse side of the card reads: "The Liberty Memorial is Kansas City's tribute to those who served in the World War in the defense of liberty and our Country. Erected from the proceeds of public subscriptions, it occupies a commanding site on Memorial Hill, overlooking Union Station, in a park 173 acres in extent. It was designed by H. Van Buren Magonigle, who was selected by a jury of eminent architects, and has been acclaimed one of the outstanding memorials of the world." The corner was laid in 1921 in the presence of General Pershing and the military leaders of the various Allied nations. In 1926, the completed structure was dedicated by President Coolidge. The two buildings pictured contain war relics and murals. Memory Hall, the east building, contains four murals. On the north wall is Pantheon de la Guerre, originally designed and painted during World War I by a group of French artists. A multi-million dollar restoration of the memorial was recently completed, and it was rededicated on Memorial Day 2003.

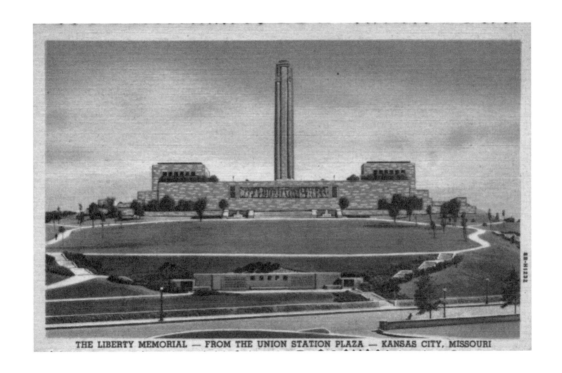

THE LIBERTY MEMORIAL — FROM THE UNION STATION PLAZA — KANSAS CITY, MISSOURI

Historic Postcards from Old Kansas City

Does this scene look familiar? Although taken over 70 years ago, such a scene was replayed throughout metropolitan Kansas City in January 2002, when the worst ice storm in the city's 150+ year history paralyzed the Metro Area. Although snowfall was minimal, ice amounts were enough to bring operations of over half the city's businesses to a halt. The scene in this postcard seems serene by comparison. Published by Jno. Straley, this card shows an automobile making its way along Cliff Drive after a snowstorm. Straley did not have to travel far to get pictures such as these, as he operated his postcard business out of his apartment at 213 N. Mersington Ave, a half-block off Gladstone Boulevard. Straley published a number of sepia-tone postcards of various Kansas City scenes during the late 1920s and early 1930s.

KANSAS CITY, mo. - CLIFF DRIVE AFTER A SNOWSTORM

Historic Postcards from Old Kansas City

Ezra Meeker wasn't particularly astute, nor did he consider himself a celebrity, but during his later years, what he singlehandedly did for the status of the Oregon Trail is nothing less than phenomenal. With his wife and infant child, Meeker set out on the Oregon Trail in 1852, settling in the Puyallup Valley of Washington State in 1853. Roughly 50 years later, in 1903-04 at the tender age of 76, Meeker decided to re-trace his steps on the old trail. This time, though, he headed east in the family wagon with his ox team. Along the way he spread the word about the old Oregon Trail, stopping and speaking wherever a crowd would gather to talk about the trail's wonderful history. In 1910, Meeker again covered the trail by wagon, financing his journey largely through the sale of commemorative postcards and books about the trail. This card shows Meeker in the Kansas City Industrial Parade on October 5, 1910. This card was never mailed and was published by Meeker himself. Following this journey, Meeker made yet another trail trek, covering its distance in a donated automobile. Then in 1924, at the age of 98, he attempted one final journey. On this trip, however, Meeker fell ill and had to get to Seattle via rail. He died shortly afterward in 1928. Due largely to Meeker's efforts, the roadbed of the trail is now considered a national historic landmark.

Ezra Meeker's Ox Team heading Industrial Parade, Kansas City, Mo.
Oct. 5, 1910

Historic Postcards from Old Kansas City

Located at 22nd Street and Brooklyn, Municipal Stadium was the home to many a professional sports team in Kansas City long before the Harry S. Truman Sports Complex was erected in 1972. Shown here on a Max Bernstein linen postcard, only a single level of seats existed early in the stadium's history. The park opened on July 3, 1923 as Muehlebach Field. It was later re-named Ruppert Stadium, Blues Stadium, then ultimately Municipal Stadium when Charlie O. Finley brought the Kansas City A's here in the mid-1950s. It was at that time the upper deck was added, increasing the seating capacity to roughly 34,000. Sadly, the stadium went the way of other vintage pro ball yards (such as Ebbetts Field, Tiger Stadium and Commisky Park) and was razed in the mid-1970s. Until very recently, it was the site of the community gardens for the surrounding area, but literally no vestiges of this historic stadium exist today.

53.-BALL PARK, KANSAS CITY, MO.

HISTORIC POSTCARDS FROM OLD KANSAS CITY

THIS POSTCARD FEATURES A VIEW OF VALENTINE ROAD, LOOKING EAST. THE PHOTO IS TAKEN FROM THE DRIVEWAY OF A RESIDENCE LOCATED WHERE VALENTINE TURNS TO THE SOUTH. ONLY ABOUT A MILE IN LENGTH, THE ROAD IS NAMED FOR P.E. VALENTINE, WHO HAD SIZABLE REAL ESTATE HOLDINGS IN KANSAS CITY AT THE TURN OF THE 20TH CENTURY. THE ROANOKE AND VALENTINE AREAS WERE POPULAR THEN BECAUSE OF THE EASY ACCESS THE NEIGHBORHOODS ENJOYED TO THE WEST BOTTOMS AND DOWNTOWN. TODAY, THE VALENTINE AREA, LIKE HISTORIC NORTHEAST, IS ENJOYING A STRONG REVITALIZATION AND CONTINUES TO BE POPULAR WITH FAMILIES WHO PREFER SETTLING IN THE HISTORIC URBAN CORE OVER THE LACKLUSTER, TREELESS BEIGE AND TAUPE SUBURBS.

VALENTINE ROAD, KANSAS CITY, MO.

HISTORIC POSTCARDS FROM OLD KANSAS CITY

THIS CARD SHOWS UNION AVENUE DURING THE CATASTROPHIC FLOOD OF 1903. WATER COVERED THE OLD "RIVER BEND" AREA AS FAR AS THE EYE COULD SEE, INCLUDING THE AREA NOW OCCUPIED BY THE DOWNTOWN AIRPORT. THOUSANDS OF PEOPLE GATHERED ON THE BLUFFS JUST WEST OF THE HANNIBAL (BROADWAY) BRIDGE OVERLOOKING THE CENTRAL INDUSTRIAL DISTRICT TO WATCH THE SWIRLING FLOOD WATERS, MUCH LIKE THE GREAT FLOODS OF 1908, 1951 AND 1993. ON JUNE 2, 1903, THE MISSOURI RIVER CRESTED AT 34.9 FEET, ALMOST 13 FEET ABOVE THE NATURAL BANK OF THE RIVER. THE FLOOD RENDERED OVER 20,000 PEOPLE HOMELESS. DAMAGE FROM THE FLOOD WAS IN THE MILLIONS OF DOLLARS AND HUNDREDS OF LIVES WERE LOST DURING THE ORDEAL. THE ONLY WORSE DISASTER WAS THE FLOOD OF 1844, WHEN WATER ROSE OVER 3 FEET HIGHER THAN IT DID IN 1903. ENGINEERS FROM THE U.S ARMY CORPS OF ENGINEERS NOW ESTIMATE THAT KANSAS CITY IS PROTECTED BY FLOOD WALLS TO OVER 43 FEET ABOVE THE RIVER'S NATURAL BANK.

Union Avenue Flood of 1903. Kansas City, Mo.

Historic Postcards from Old Kansas City

The old A-S-B bridge is pictured on this postcard, published by Elite Postcard Company of Kansas City, Missouri (A-S-B stands for Armour, Swift & Burlington). It shows the bridge while it was still under construction in the early 1900s and identifies the span as the "North Kansas City Bridge." The card was mailed in 1915, four years after the bridge was completed. At that time only the upper level of the structure had been completed when the picture was made. Trains ran on the lower level of the structure. Until the building of the bridge, ferry boats were the primary mode of transportation across the river. Tolls charged to cross the bridge mirrored those previously charged by the ferry: foot passengers, 5 cents; bicycle and rider, 5 cents; horse and rider, 10 cents; horses, mules and cattle per head, 10 cents; sheep, hogs and calves per head, 3 cents; one-horse vehicle, 20 cents; two-horse vehicle, 25 cents; three-horse vehicle, 30 cents; four-horse vehicle, 35 cents; automobile, one seat, 20 cents; automobile, two-seat, 25 cents; trucks, 35 cents; circus and menagerie wagons, 40 cents; threshing machines, 40 cents; extra passengers on vehicles, 5 cents. The tolls were discontinued in 1927. The bridge opened a new territory for Kansas City, with easy access to towns north of the river, such as North Kansas City, Liberty, Excelsior Springs, Richmond, Carrollton, Chillicothe, Plattsburg, Cameron, Hamilton, Platte City and St. Joseph.

North Kansas City Bridge.
Kansas City, Mo

HISTORIC POSTCARDS FROM OLD KANSAS CITY

ON FRIDAY, JULY 13, 1951, KANSAS CITY EXPERIENCED ITS WORST NATURAL DISASTER TO DATE. THE KAW RIVER, SWOLLEN BY HEAVY RAINS, ROSE TO UNPRECEDENTED HEIGHTS, FLOODING THE RICH INDUSTRIAL DISTRICT, AS WELL AS THE ARMOURDALE AND ARGENTINE RESIDENTIAL DISTRICTS. THIS PHOTO SHOWS THE 12TH STREET VIADUCT AND WAREHOUSES INUNDATED BY FLOODWATERS IN THE CENTRAL INDUSTRIAL DISTRICT. ALMOST 11 SQUARE MILES LAY UNDER WATER AND THOUSANDS OF HOGS AND CATTLE WERE SWEPT AWAY BY THE TURBULENT WATERS OF THE KANSAS. FIRE BROKE OUT IN THE OILY WATERS AND SPREAD TO THE HUGE PETROLEUM STORAGE TANKS ALONG SOUTHWEST BOULEVARD, WREAKING EVEN MORE HAVOC ON THE ALREADY PARALYZED AREA. THE DISASTER COST CLOSE TO ONE BILLION IN 1951 DOLLARS AND TOOK ALMOST SEVEN MONTHS TO CLEAN UP. NOTED ARTISTS NORMAN ROCKWELL AND JOHN ATHERTON WERE COMMISSIONED BY HALLMARK CHIEF JOYCE HALL TO DO A PAINTING SIGNIFYING THE "KANSAS CITY SPIRIT." YOU MAY SEE IT AND OTHER WORKS ON DISPLAY AT THE HALLMARK VISITORS CENTER IN CROWN CENTER.

12TH STREET VIADUCT, FLOOD OF 1951

Historic Postcards from Old Kansas City

Built in the mid-1930s at a cost of roughly one million dollars, the Hall of Waters was the capstone to the Excelsior Springs resort facilities. This card shows a view from the west and proclaims "America's Haven of Health." A description on the rear of the card indicates, "In the Hall of Waters is included a beautiful dispensary called the Hall of Springs where a unique variety of mineral waters is served: iron, manganese, saline laxative waters, soda bicarbonate waters and calcium water. The waters are also bottled in a model bottling plant." Today, the Hall of Waters is enjoying a renaissance of some magnitude. Therapeutic massage, bubble tubs, and light and steam baths are all offered in the historic setting of this wonderful Art Deco building. After almost 70 years of service, the Hall of Waters is still the "World's Longest Water Bar."

HALL OF WATERS — AMERICA'S HAVEN OF HEALTH — EXCELSIOR SPRINGS, MO.

Historic Postcards from Old Kansas City

Two street cars dominate the scene on this postcard published by Max Bernstein in the late teens or early 1920s. Several automobiles are in view, but no horse-and-buggy traffic. Stores and shops display large overhanging signs; among them is Federman's Drug Store at 11th and Walnut, a site later occupied by Woolf Brothers. Farther along are signs for the Olney Music Company and Household Fair. On the right is a sign designating the Altman Building entrance with a hand pointing the way. The Commerce Trust Company is in the center background. The 1918 city directory lists these banks on the block as well: Commerce Trust Co., 10th and Walnut; Commonwealth National Bank, northwest corner of Ninth and Walnut; Fidelity Trust Co., southeast corner of Ninth and Walnut; Missouri Savings Association Bank, 920 Walnut; National Fidelity Bank of New York, 711 Republic Building; National City Bank, 912-914 Walnut; National Reserve Bank of Kansas City, southwest corner of 10th and Walnut; State Bank of Kansas City, 921 Walnut; and the Western Exchange Bank, 900 Walnut Ave.

Walnut Street, North from 12th St., Kansas City, Mo.

HISTORIC POSTCARDS FROM OLD KANSAS CITY

THIS HISTORIC POSTCARD WAS PUBLISHED BY THE WEBB FREYSCHLAG MERCANTILE COMPANY AND SHOWS THE "NEW" CONVENTION HALL AS IT LOOKED UPON ITS RE-DEDICATION IN 1900. THE BUILDING SHOWN HERE HOUSED TWO NATIONAL POLITICAL CONVENTIONS. DURING THE CONVENTION OF 1900, THE DEMOCRATS MET AND NOMINATED WILLIAM JENNINGS BRYAN FOR PRESIDENT. IN 1928, REPUBLICANS CONVENED IN CONVENTION HALL AND CHOSE HERBERT HOOVER AS THEIR NOMINEE. THE HALL WAS BUILT IN 90 DAYS WHEN THE FIRST CONVENTION HALL, ERECTED IN 1899, BURNED ON APRIL 4, 1900. WITH THE DEMOCRATS DUE TO MEET THERE IN LESS THAN 100 DAYS, SPIRITED PLEDGES TOWARD REBUILDING THE STRUCTURE WERE MADE EVEN AS FIRE CONTINUED TO RAGE. THE RE-OPENING OF THE NEWLY CONSTRUCTED FACILITY, WHEN THE HALL WAS READY IN TIME FOR THE DEMOCRATIC CONVENTION OF 1900, WAS CALLED "KANSAS CITY'S FINEST HOUR." CONVENTION HALL SERVED UNTIL THE PRESENT MUNICIPAL AUDITORIUM WAS COMPLETED IN 1935. THE STRUCTURE WAS THEN RAZED AND THE AUDITORIUM GARAGE WAS CONSTRUCTED UNDERGROUND ON THE SITE.

168 – Convention Hall, Kansas City, Mo.

Historic Postcards from Old Kansas City

The structure, designed by Jarvis Hunt, replaced a depot on Union Avenue in the West Bottoms. At the time it was built it was the largest passenger station in the world, apart from New York City's Grand Central and Pennsylvania stations. The grounds cost $44 million, with the depot itself costing roughly $6 million. "The wide plaza at the entrance 53 years ago has become parking space for automobiles. Otherwise, the exterior is little changed. But as rail lines discontinued passenger service, the cathedral-like lobbies are empty much of the time, and city and terminal officials look for new uses for this grand and sturdy example of classic architecture." Such was the description given by Mrs. Sam Ray for her Kansas City Star column on May 4, 1968. It would be another 19 years until train service was totally discontinued at the station; a single bulb left burning in a window was caught in a striking photo by one of the passengers on the last train out. Today Union Station is a bustling hub in the heart of the re-emerging Freight House District. This card was published by Max Bernstein and was never mailed.

New Union Station, Kansas City, Mo.
Cost of Building $6,000,000.00.
Cost of Terminal $44,000,000.00.

From Drawing by Teachenor-Bartberger Eng. Co., Kansas City, Mo.

Historic Postcards from Old Kansas City

The red brick building shown in this postcard, built in 1895 on the banks of the Kansas River, was the third such building of its kind to serve as the Kansas City Livestock Exchange. Located at 16th street & State Line, the building shown here was actually two blocks West of the present Livestock Exchange building. A strip of colored tile was laid across the floor of the lobby indicating the line between Kansas & Missouri. Most of the structure was in Kansas. The "new" building was built entirely in Missouri. During the great flood of 1903, hogs and cattle were driven into the elevated chutes built over the stockyards. The upper floors of the exchange building were actually used to hold animals until flood waters subsided. Flood damage to the old facility (pictured here) was so extensive that the new facility was built. The Hog & Sheep house occupied the site of the old building for a time. The new building was considered the finest of its kind anywhere, and still remains a testament to the height of the livestock trade in Kansas City. Sadly, the Stockyards were razed entirely in the early 1990s. The only indication of the Stockyards that were once the second largest in the world is a remnant of the foundation wall unearthed along the East bank of the Kaw River.

EXCHANGE BLDG. UNION STOCK YARDS, KANSAS CITY, MO.

HISTORIC POSTCARDS FROM OLD KANSAS CITY

THIS IS A BLACK-AND-WHITE, UNDIVIDED BACK POSTCARD, PUBLISHED BY THE SOUTHWEST NEWS COMPANY OF KANSAS CITY, MISSOURI. IT WAS MAILED TO MISS LIZZIE DORNES OF SABETHA, KAN. ON NOV. 9, 1907. THE GREETING ON THE FRONT READS: "HERE'S TO YOUR POST CARD ALBUM. WE ARE JUST TWO BLOCKS AWAY FROM HERE, MARJORIE TENNELL." THIS CARD SHOWS A FEW EARLY AUTOMOBILES ALONG THE SIDE OF MAIN STREET, AS WELL AS A STREETCAR APPROACHING THE NINTH, MAIN AND DELAWARE INTERSECTIONS. DELAWARE CAN BE SEEN MERGING INTO MAIN ON THE LEFT. JUDGING FROM THE SHADOWS OF THE AWNINGS AND THE BUILDINGS, THIS PHOTOGRAPH WAS TAKEN VERY CLOSE TO MID-DAY. THE BUILDING PARTLY SEEN AT THE RIGHT SIDE OF THE CARD IS VAUGHAN'S OLD DIAMOND BUILDING. THIS WEDGE-SHAPED STRUCTURE FACED "THE JUNCTION," WHERE SEVERAL STREET CAR LINES CAME TOGETHER AT NINTH, MAIN AND DELAWARE STREETS. AT THE TIME, THE JUNCTION WAS REPUTED TO BE KANSAS CITY'S BUSIEST INTERSECTION. TODAY THIS AREA IS MARKED BY A 30-FOOT HIGH MONUMENT, "MUSE OF THE MISSOURI." IT WAS PRESENTED TO THE CITY BY MR. AND MRS. JAMES KEMPER, SR. IN HONOR OF THEIR SON, LT. DAVID W. KEMPER, WHO WAS KILLED IN ACTION IN ITALY DURING WORLD WAR II.

Main Street South from 8th St. Kansas City, Mo.

Historic Postcards from Old Kansas City

Labeled "The Tower on West Terrace, Kansas City, Missouri," this card shows the new design implemented by landscape architect George Kessler in his massive overhaul of the West Bluffs. Once a shabby, overgrown hill covered with shacks and scrub brush, the bluffs became Kessler's flagship project for Kansas City's then fledgling Park Board. The new design incorporated twin "cupola" style towers of native limestone overlooking the West Bottoms. A formidable wall and a set of stairs cascaded downward to Kersey Coates Drive. A fountain with benches lay inside the inlet at the foot of the stairs. Kessler was lauded for his undertaking and was ultimately responsible for the design of Kansas City's initial boulevard system, as well as the buildings in many parks. This card was mailed to Mrs. J.C. Kanturek of Rosedale, Kan., now incorporated into Kansas City, Kan. Mailed on September 11, 1913 from Westport Station, it reads: "Will be over a week from Sunday. I wasn't to go home this coming Sunday. I suppose may get to your place all right. I haven't been home since I came out here. Love, your sister, Dora."

Tower on West Terrace, Kansas City, Mo.

P14272

HISTORIC POSTCARDS FROM OLD KANSAS CITY

THIS CARD FEATURES THE BRIDGE OVER THE BLUE RIVER AT INDEPENDENCE AVENUE. PUBLISHED EXPRESSLY FOR S.H. KNOX, THIS CARD SHOWS THE HIGH BRIDGE AND NUMEROUS PEOPLE OVERLOOKING THE PLACID SCENE BELOW. EARLY IN THE LAST CENTURY, THE BLUE RIVER WAS CONSIDERED THE PLAYGROUND OF KANSAS CITY, HOME TO HOUSE-BOATS AND RENTAL CRAFT. THE BOATS WERE USED FOR PICNICS OR AS SUMMER HOMES FROM APRIL THROUGH LABOR DAY. THERE WAS ALSO A COMMUNITY OF SUMMER COTTAGES NEARBY, THE LAST OF WHICH WAS RECENTLY DEMOLISHED. TODAY THE RIVER LOOKS NOTHING LIKE THE SCENE SHOWN HERE. THE BLUE RIVER FLOOD CONTROL PROJECT HAS RE-ROUTED THE RIVER IN SOME AREAS, AND THE SHADY RIVERBANKS HAVE BEEN REPLACED BY A HUGE CONCRETE BASIN BETWEEN BRUSH CREEK AND THE MISSOURI RIVER. THIS CARD WAS SENT TO MRS. E.H. TRUDEAU OF CHASE COUNTY, KAN. IT WAS MAILED AUGUST 23, 1912.

Blue River at Independence Avenue, Kansas City, Mo.

Historic Postcards from Old Kansas City

This historic postcard, published by the Valentine Souvenir company of New York, shows a "scene on the Missouri River near Kansas City, Missouri." This view could be anywhere along the river in our region, but was probably taken looking west back toward Kansas City. This is evident as there are some buildings faintly outlined in the center right of the card. The river has long been a source of commerce for our town, and continues to remain so today. Take a few minutes to drive to our City Market area, and hike down to what remains of Main street. From here you can view the foundations of what was once the Gillis House Hotel, one of the very first buildings built in the then-burgeoning frontier "Town of Kansas."

Scene on
the Missouri River,
near Kansas City, Mo.

HISTORIC POSTCARDS FROM OLD KANSAS CITY

THIS 3-ACRE LAKE SHOWN ON THIS CARD, PUBLISHED BY THE ELITE POSTCARD COMPANY OF KANSAS CITY, WAS ONCE PART OF AN AREA CALLED "VINEGAR HILL." ONCE POPULATED BY SHACKS, SHANTIES AND LEAN-TOS, THE AREA IS NOW THE SITE OF BEAUTIFUL PENN VALLEY PARK. LAND ACQUISITION FOR THE PARK BEGAN IN 1900 AND CONTINUED UNTIL 1926, WHEN ALMOST 176 ACRES HAD BEEN SECURED. NOTED LANDSCAPE ARCHITECT GEORGE E. KESSLER OVERSAW THE CONSTRUCTION OF THE PARK, AND WAS ULTIMATELY RESPONSIBLE FOR THE DESIGN OF MUCH OF KANSAS CITY'S GROWING PARKS & BOULEVARDS SYSTEM. KESSLER WORK AS LANDSCAPE ARCHITECT WITH THE PARK BOARD STARTED IN 1892, AND PLANS LAID THEN CONTINUED THROUGH THE YEARS AS PART OF THE "KANSAS CITY PLAN." KESSLER ENCOUNTERED MUCH OPPOSITION TO HIS AMBITIOUS PLANS, BUT HE WAS FIRMLY BACKED BY THE PARK BOARD PRESIDENT, A. R. MEYER, AND WILLIAM ROCKHILL NELSON, PUBLISHER AND OWNER OF THE KANSAS CITY STAR. PENN VALLEY PARK LIES IN WHAT IS NOW CONSIDERED "MIDTOWN" KANSAS CITY. IN 1906, KANSAS CITY WAS AWARDED SECOND PLACE AMONG MAJOR CITIES OF THE U. S. FOR ITS "COMPREHENSIVE, CONNECTED AND COMPLETED PARK AND BOULEVARD SYSTEM." MUCH CREDIT FOR THE HONOR WENT TO GEORGE KESSLER. PENN VALLEY PARK LIES ROUGHLY BETWEEN 31ST STREET TO PERSHING ROAD, AND WYONDOTTE TO SUMMIT.

Penn Valley Park, Kansas City, Mo.

Historic Postcards from Old Kansas City

The corner of Independence and Gladstone Boulevards hasn't always been made of grocery stores and apartment buildings as this postcard form 1908 shows. This view, "looking North on Gladstone Blvd. from Independence," shows a stark contrast to what exists today. At the center of the picture are the two primary modes of transportation of the day. Automobiles, in their infancy at this time, shared the roadway with horses and buggies. A number of the homes on Gladstone Boulevard have carriage houses still in use today as homes or car garages. In the easement are the elm trees planted by the city's Parks Department, in accordance with landscape architect George Kessler's design. Unfortunately, most of these trees were wiped out in the 1920s when Dutch elm disease ravaged the area. A majority of the houses shown still stand today. Those on the right were converted to apartments long ago and remain so today. The home on the left is still a single family home and is presently listed with a real estate company.

Gladstone Blvd. North from Independence Ave., Kansas City, Mo.

Historic Postcards from Old Kansas City

Published in 1907, this divided back postcard shows "Seeing Kansas City" streetcar Number 102 on Cliff Drive. In all actuality, the location of the streetcar is on Lexington Avenue, just west of the new bridge running over what is now Chestnut Trafficway. Cliff Drive can be seen far below where the streetcar tracks actually ran. The "Seeing Kansas City" streetcars were caught outside the Owl Drug Store on Main Street and traveled throughout the city, mainly along the city's acclaimed system of boulevards and parks. Advertisements on the coach indicate that the route is 25 miles in length and the office can be reached by "both phones, 596, Main." Standing outside the car, at the front corner, is the conductor, complete with a megaphone so highlights of the sightseeing tour can be "broadcast" to the patrons in the streetcar. The Motorman can be seen directly behind the front glass. The card was sent to Mrs F.H. Zeigler of Harrisonville, Missouri on September 13, 1907. The note reads, "Had a short note from Elmer saying Aunt Isema was able to talk some now, and they were hopeful of her getting better. Elmer's three year old boy got his leg broken few weeks ago. Hope you are well. Sincerely, Irene."

On Cliff Drive, Kansas City, Mo.

Historic Postcards from Old Kansas City

On April 2, 1917, President Woodrow Wilson called Congress to declare a state of war between the United States and the Imperial German Government. With that declaration, the American Red Cross sprang into action. During the war years, the Red Cross maintained a canteen at Union Station, allowing soldiers to send postcards home or to loved ones. Other services included hot drinks and hospitality furnished by Red Cross volunteers. This card, published by the American Red Cross, shows the Canteen at Union Station in Kansas City, Missouri. Behind the staff posed for the picture is a large "information bureau" with other area services listed, such as the YMCA at 10th and Oak. This card was sent to Mrs. P.L. Spencer of Jersey City, New Jersey on July 26, 1919. It reads: "Dear Mother, I am still at camp Merritt. Will write you later. Lots of love to all, Vester."

RED CROSS CANTEEN, UNION STATION, KANSAS CITY, MO.

Historic Postcards from Old Kansas City

"The new home of The F. Warner Karling Furniture Company, 15th and Olive Streets, Kansas City, Mo." This building looks much the same now as it did when this card was published by the Hall Brothers Company in the early 1920s. Gaines Furniture Outlet currently occupies the building and has for the past 18 years. According to Robert Gaines, prior to their furniture operation, the building housed a division of the Social Security Administration. Before that, Davidow's Furniture Company occupied the space. The Karling name is still intact, laid in mosiac tile at the front door.

The New Home of the
F. Warner Karling Furniture Company,
15th and Olive Streets, Kansas City, Mo.

Historic Postcards from Old Kansas City

Built in 1914 by Howard Vrooman and designed by Owens & Payson, Architects, the St. Regis was one of Kansas City's premier addresses. Located at the northeast corner of Linwood Boulevard and the Paseo, the hotel was home to a number of prominent Kansas City families of the day, including steel magnate Theodore Gary, who occupied the largest suite in the hotel. It was said that the ballroom on the 9th floor was the highest point in Kansas City. Throughout the lobby, one can see the finest in appointments, including tapestries on the walls, fine silk curtains, a grand piano, and French Sienna marble lining the walls and staircases. Little of the lobby as it is shown remains today. While the stately columns and their intricate dentilwork remain, a rental office occupies a portion of the first floor and the open space has been subdivided into various areas more conducive to apartment living. This postcard was published by the Fergason Postcard Company of Waterloo, Iowa.

LOBBY, THE ST. REGIS.
THE PASEO AT LINWOOD BLD., KANSAS CITY, MO.

Historic Postcards from Old Kansas City

This extremely rare, Real Photo Postcard published by the North American Postcard Company of Kansas City, Missouri, shows the Passantino Bros. Funeral Home, located at 2117 Independence Boulevard. Founded in 1930 by brothers Charles, George and Rosario Passantino, the family began a tradition of offering personal, professional and compassionate service, with special attention to each family they served. According to the late Leonard "Bull" Passantino (Northeast High School class of 1945), the Cadillac hearse shown in the picture under the porte-cochere was a huge V-12 that "rattled the whole house" when it idled. An American Legion placard stands in the window indicating that part of the family was serving in the armed forces. The converted Independence Boulevard mansion is still home to Passantino Bros. today, 73 years after its founding.

PASSANTINO FUNERAL HOME
2117 INDEP. AVE. (BLVD.)
~ 1933 ~

ABOUT THE EDITOR

MICHAEL BUSHNELL PUBLISHES <u>THE NORTHEAST NEWS</u>, A WEEKLY COMMUNITY NEWSPAPER SERVING THE HISTORIC NORTHEAST AREA OF KANSAS CITY, MO. HE AND HIS WIFE, CHRISTINE, PURCHASED THE PAPER IN 1998 AND QUICKLY CONVERTED IT FROM A WEEKLY TABLOID SHOPPER TO A VIABLE COMMUNITY NEWS SOURCE FOR THE NORTHEAST AREA. AS PART OF THAT TRANSITION, PICTURES OF OLD KANSAS CITY POSTCARDS FROM MICHAEL'S COLLECTION WERE PUBLISHED EACH WEEK, OFFERING A VIEW OF THE EARLY HISTORY OF HISTORIC NORTHEAST, AS WELL AS KANSAS CITY AS A WHOLE. THIS BOOK, A COMPILATION OF THE FIRST FOUR YEARS OF POSTCARDS PUBLISHED IN <u>THE NORTHEAST NEWS</u>, IS MICHAEL'S FIRST WORK. MICHAEL AND CHRIS LIVE IN THE HEART OF THE SCARRITT RENAISSANCE NEIGHBORHOOD IN A RESTORED CRAFTSMAN SHIRTWAIST HOME WITH THEIR THREE DOGS, TODD, ABBEY AND BUNNY (THE NORTHEAST NEWS-HOUND!). AMONG OTHER PURSUITS, INCLUDING COLLECTING OLD KANSAS CITY POSTCARDS, MICHAEL IS ACTIVE IN THE SCARRITT RENAISSANCE NEIGHBORHOOD ASSOCIATION, MELROSE UNITED METHODIST CHURCH, NEWHOUSE DOMESTIC VIOLENCE SHELTER, AND THE GREATER KANSAS CITY CHAPTER OF H.O.G. (HARLEY OWNERS GROUP).